MIDLOTHIAN PUBLIC LIBRARY

3 1614 00185 6377

W9-CNO-386

Rank It!

DINOSAURS

MEGAN COOLEY PETERSON

BRIDGEVIEW PUBLIC LIBRARY
7840 S. KENTON AVENUE
BRIDGEVIEW, IL 60455

BLACK
RABBIT
BOOKS

Bolt is published by Black Rabbit Books
P.O. Box 3263, Mankato, Minnesota, 56002.
www.blackrabbitbooks.com
Copyright © 2017 Black Rabbit Books

Design and Production by Michael Sellner
Photo Research by Rhonda Milbrett

All rights reserved. No part of this book may be reproduced in any
form without written permission from the publisher.

Library of Congress Control Number: 2015954676

HC ISBN: 978-1-68072-060-0   PB ISBN: 978-1-68072-266-6

Printed in the United States at CG Book Printers,
North Mankato, Minnesota, 56003. PO #1791 4/16

Web addresses included in this book were working and appropriate
at the time of publication. The publisher is not responsible for broken
or changed links.

E
56719
PET

Image Credits
Alamy: Stocktrek Imag-
es, Inc., 15; Dreamstime: Petr
Malohlava, 20; Masato Hattori: Cover,
4–5, 6, 9, 10–11, 12, 14, 26–27; Mohamad
Haghani: 8, 19; Shutterstock: Airin.dizain,
28 (Brachiosaurus); Catmando, 28 (Giganotosaurus); dkvektor, 28 (Spinosaurus); Donnay
Style, 13, 25; Elenarts, 23; Herschel Hoffmeyer,
24; metha1819, 31; Michael Rosskothen, 23, 27;
Roger Hall, 3; SAHACHAT SANEHA, Back Cover,
1; Seregraff, 32; Vital9s, 6, 9, 15, 21, 22 (paw)
Every effort has been made to contact copyright holders for material reproduced
in this book. Any omissions will be
rectified in subsequent printings
if notice is given to the
publisher.

CONTENTS

CHAPTER 1

When DINOSAURS Walked the Earth

Dinosaurs lived between 230 million and 65 million years ago. Some had sharp teeth. Others had **beaks** and ate bugs.

What was the tallest dinosaur? Which dinosaur would win a race? Turn the page, and see where your favorite dinosaurs rank.

RANK IT!

30 FEET
(9 M)
ESTIMATED LENGTH

3,800 POUNDS
(1,724 KG)
ESTIMATED WEIGHT

20 MILES
(32 KM)
PER HOUR
ESTIMATED
SPEED

16.5 FEET
(5 M)
ESTIMATED HEIGHT

CHAPTER 2

The DINOS

Allosaurus
(al-oh-SAW-rus)

means "Different Lizard"

You wouldn't want to mess with Allosaurus. It was a fierce fighter. Allosaurus used its strong neck to drive its teeth into **prey**. Then it ripped flesh from the bone.

Ankylosaurus
(ang-ki-lo-SAW-rus)

means "Fused Lizard"

Ankylosaurus lived in forests in North America. Plates in its skin kept this plant eater safe from **predators**.

35 FEET ESTIMATED LENGTH (11 M)	4 FEET (1 M) ESTIMATED HEIGHT
10,000 POUNDS (4,536 KG) ESTIMATED WEIGHT	6 MILES (10 KM) PER HOUR ESTIMATED SPEED

Brachiosaurus
(brak-ee-uh-SAW-rus)
means "Arm Lizard"

Brachiosaurus towered over other dinosaurs. Like a giraffe, Brachiosaurus had a long neck. Its neck made up about half its total length. Brachiosaurus had 52 spoon-shaped teeth. These teeth were perfect for pulling leaves from branches.

RANK IT!

85 FEET
(26 M)
ESTIMATED LENGTH

120,000 POUNDS
(54,431 KG)
ESTIMATED WEIGHT

10 MILES
(16 KM)
PER HOUR
ESTIMATED SPEED

50 FEET
(15 M)
ESTIMATED HEIGHT

MESOZOIC ERA

Triassic Period	Jurassic Period
(251-199 million years ago)	(199-145 million years ago)
	Allosaurus
	Brachiosaurus
	Stegosaurus

PERIOD	Triassic	Jurassic
MILLIONS OF YEARS AGO	251 199	145

Cretaceous Period
(145-65 million years ago)

Ankylosaurus
Giganotosaurus
Microraptor
Ornithomimus
Spinosaurus
Triceratops
Tyrannosaurus Rex
Velociraptor

Cretaceous

Age of Mammals

145   65   PRESENT

Giganotosaurus
(gig-an-o-toe-SAW-rus)

means "Giant Southern Reptile"

Giganotosaurus roamed the **plains** and forests of Argentina. This hunter had teeth 8 inches (20 centimeters) long. Each tooth was shaped like a knife. Giganotosaurus' body was huge. But its brain was only about the size of a banana!

45 FEET
(14 M)
ESTIMATED
LENGTH

18,000 POUNDS
(8,165 KG)
ESTIMATED
WEIGHT

23 FEET
(7 M)
ESTIMATED
HEIGHT

31 MILES
(50 KM)
PER HOUR
ESTIMATED
SPEED

RANK IT!

Microraptor
(MYK-row-rap-tuhr)

means "Small Thief"

Microraptor was a small dinosaur.
It was only the size of a turkey. It spread
out its limbs to glide between trees.

RANK IT!

	ESTIMATED LENGTH		ESTIMATED HEIGHT
2 FEET (1 M)		1 FOOT (.3 M)	

3 POUNDS (1 KG) ESTIMATED WEIGHT	33 MILES (53 KM) PER HOUR	ESTIMATED SPEED

Ornithomimus
(or-ni-thuh-MY-mus)

means "Bird Mimic"

Ornithomimus looked like an ostrich. It had a small head and long neck. Instead of teeth, Ornithomimus had a sharp beak. It ate bugs and leaves. This speedy dinosaur darted through forests in North America.

RANK IT!

11.5 FEET
(4 M)
ESTIMATED LENGTH

350 POUNDS
(159 KG)
ESTIMATED WEIGHT

43 MILES
(69 KM)
PER HOUR
ESTIMATED SPEED

8 FEET
(2 M)
ESTIMATED HEIGHT

WHERE DINOSAURS LIVED

Dinosaur **fossils** have been found all over the world. Here are a few of the top sites.

DINOSAUR NATIONAL MONUMENT
in the western United States

VALLE DE LA LUNA
in Argentina

FLAMING CLIFFS
in Mongolia

DASHANPU FORMATION
in eastern China

DINOSAUR COVE
in Australia

Spinosaurus
(SPI-nuh-sawr-us)

means "Spined Reptile"

Spinosaurus may have been the only dinosaur to live in water. This hunter scooped up fish and sharks with crocodile-like jaws. It had webbed back feet.

Spinosaurus did not have sharp teeth. Its teeth were shaped like cones to trap fish. A tall **sail** grew on its back.

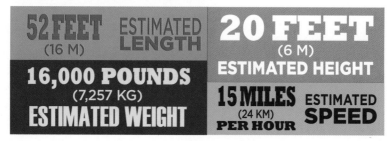

52 FEET (16 M) ESTIMATED LENGTH	20 FEET (6 M) ESTIMATED HEIGHT
16,000 POUNDS (7,257 KG) ESTIMATED WEIGHT	15 MILES (24 KM) PER HOUR ESTIMATED SPEED

Some say Stegosaurus was one of the dumbest dinosaurs. Its brain was only about the size of a hot dog.

Stegosaurus
(steg-uh-SAW-rus)

means "Covered Lizard"

Stegosaurus was a master of **armor**. This dinosaur had 17 pointed plates on its back. It also had armored lumps in its neck. These lumps protected Stegosaurus from dinosaurs that bit its throat.

Stegosaurus was too slow to run from danger. This plant eater swung its spiked tail at enemies.

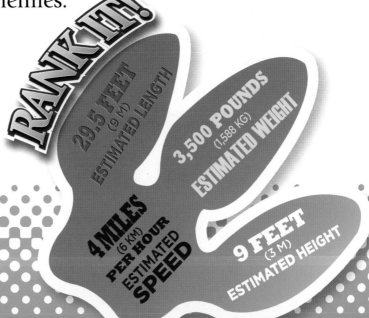

RANK IT!

29.5 FEET
(9 M)
ESTIMATED LENGTH

3,500 POUNDS
(1,588 KG)
ESTIMATED WEIGHT

4 MILES
(6 KM)
PER HOUR
ESTIMATED SPEED

9 FEET
(3 M)
ESTIMATED HEIGHT

Triceratops
(tri-SAYR-uh-tops)
means "Three-Horned Face"

Triceratops was built like a rhino.
It had two long horns on its brow.
One short horn grew on its nose.
A bony frill protected this plant eater's
neck. Triceratops used its horns to
bash Tyrannosaurus Rex.

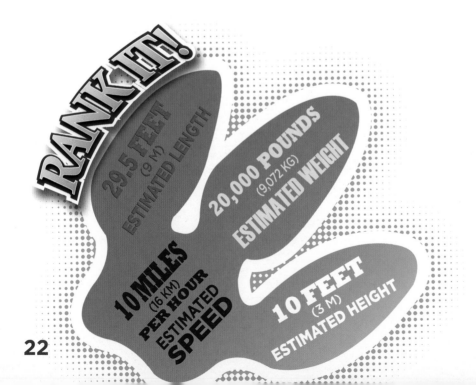

RANK IT!

29.5 FEET
(9 M)
ESTIMATED LENGTH

20,000 POUNDS
(9,072 KG)
ESTIMATED WEIGHT

10 MILES
(16 KM)
PER HOUR
ESTIMATED SPEED

10 FEET
(3 M)
ESTIMATED HEIGHT

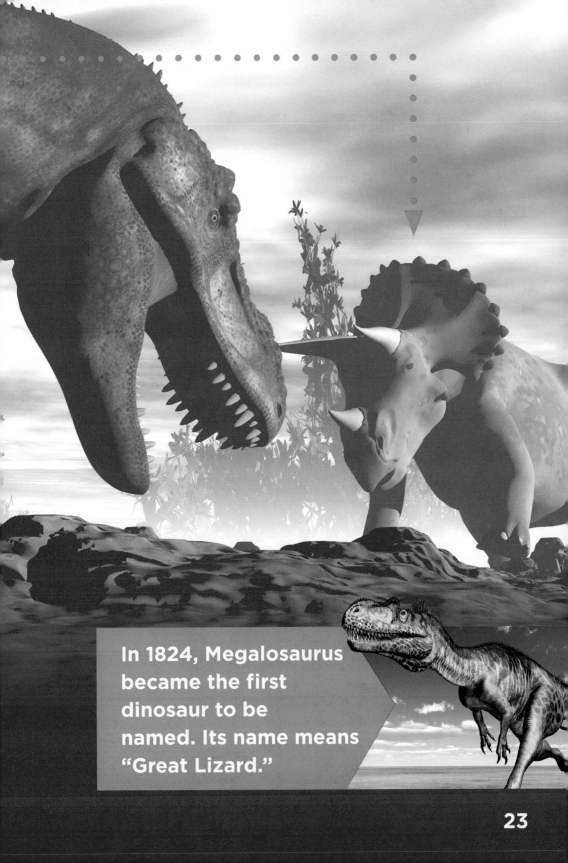

In 1824, Megalosaurus became the first dinosaur to be named. Its name means "Great Lizard."

Tyrannosaurus Rex

(ti-RAN-uh-sawr-uhs REKS) **means "King of the Tyrant Lizards"**

Tyrannosaurus rex struck fear into other dinosaurs. Its 60 knifelike teeth could slice through skin and crush bone. Some teeth grew up to 13 inches (33 cm) long! When it wasn't hunting, T. rex ate dead animals.

40 FEET (12 M) ESTIMATED LENGTH

18,000 POUNDS (8,165 KG) ESTIMATED WEIGHT

13 FEET (4 M) ESTIMATED HEIGHT

25 MILES (40 KM) PER HOUR ESTIMATED SPEED

RANK IT!

Velociraptor
(veh-LAW-sih-rap-tur)

means "Speedy Thief"

Velociraptor was a swift hunter. It ran through the deserts of Asia. Velociraptor's long, stiff tail helped it make quick turns to catch prey. Feathers covered this dinosaur, but it could not fly.

RANK IT!

7 FEET (2 M) ESTIMATED LENGTH

2 FEET (1 M) ESTIMATED HEIGHT

33 POUNDS (15 KG) ESTIMATED WEIGHT

40 MILES (64 KM) PER HOUR ESTIMATED SPEED

Velociraptors starred in the movie *Jurassic Park*. But they weren't accurate. Moviemakers made Velociraptors look and act like Deinonychuses. Deinonychuses were larger relatives of Velociraptors.

CHAPTER 3

Weight

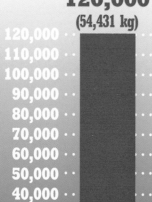

120,000
(54,431 kg)

POUNDS				
120,000				
110,000				
100,000				
90,000				
80,000				
70,000				
60,000				
50,000				
40,000				
30,000				
20,000				
10,000				
0				

20,000
(9,072 kg)

18,000
(8,165 kg)

18,000
(8,165 kg)

16,000
(7,257 kg)

Brachiosaurus   Triceratops   Giganotosaurus   T. rex   Spinosaurus

Length

Brachiosaurus
85 feet
(26 m)

Spinosaurus
52 feet
(16 m)

Giganotosaurus
45 feet
(14 m)

28

RANK IT!

Check out how your favorites stack up.

10,000 (4,536 kg)	3,800 (1,724 kg)	3,500 (1,588 kg)	350 (159 kg)	33 (15 kg)	3 (1 kg)
Ankylosaurus	Allosaurus	Stegosaurus	Ornithomimus	Velociraptor	Microraptor

HEIGHT

50 feet (15 m)	23 feet (7 m)	20 feet (6 m)
Brachiosaurus	Giganotosaurus	Spinosaurus

ORNITHOMIMUS 43 miles (69 km) per hour **VELOCIRAPTOR** 40 miles (64 km) per hour **MICRORAPTOR** 33 miles (53 km) per hour

GLOSSARY

armor (AR-muhr)—a protective outer layer

beak (BEEK)—the hard front part of the mouth of birds and some dinosaurs

era (AYR-uh)—a period of time

fossil (FAH-sul)—the remains or traces of plants and animals that are preserved as rock

plain (PLAYN)—a stretch of nearly treeless country

predator (PRED-uh-tuhr)—an animal that eats other animals

prey (PRAY)—an animal hunted or killed for food

sail (SAYL)—a bony growth used to regulate body heat and warn other dinosaurs

BOOKS

Staunton, Joseph. *Meat-Eating Dinosaurs.* Discover the Dinosaurs. Mankato, MN: Amicus, 2011.

West, David. *Dinosaurs of the Jurassic.* Prehistoric! Mankato, MN: Smart Apple Media, 2015.

Woodward, John. *Dinosaur!: Dinosaurs and Other Amazing Prehistoric Creatures as You've Never Seen Them Before.* New York: DK Publishing, 2014.

WEBSITES

Dinosaurs
discoverykids.com/category/dinosaurs/

Dinosaurs for Kids
www.kidsdinos.com

PBS Kids: Dinosaur Games
pbskids.org/games/dinosaur/

INDEX